My Little Golden Book About
GIRAFFES

W0114451

The editors would like to thank Kim Garcia Szawan, Animal Care Manager, Woodland Park Zoo, for her assistance in the preparation of this book.

BY BONNIE BADER · ILLUSTRATED BY STEPH LABERIS

A GOLDEN BOOK • NEW YORK

Golden Books
An imprint of Random House Children's Books
A division of Penguin Random House LLC
1745 Broadway, New York, NY 10019
penguinrandomhouse.com
rhcbooks.com
Text copyright © 2025 by Bonnie Bader
Cover and interior illustrations copyright © 2025 by Steph Laberis
Golden Books, A Golden Book, A Little Golden Book, the G colophon, and the distinctive
gold spine are registered trademarks of Penguin Random House LLC.
Library of Congress Control Number: 2024945610
ISBN 978-0-593-89806-2 (trade) — ISBN 978-0-593-89807-9 (ebook)
Manufactured in the United States of America
10 9 8 7 6 5 4 3 2 1
EU Contact: Penguin Random House Ireland, 32 Nassau Street, Dublin D02 YH68.
https://eu-contact.penguin.ie.

Say hello to the world's tallest land animal: **the giraffe**.

Just about everything on a giraffe is big. Its legs are about six feet long. Its neck stretches about six feet high. Male giraffes can grow as tall as eighteen feet—that's tall enough to peek into a window on the second floor of a house! Female giraffes can grow up to fourteen feet.

A giraffe's tongue is also big, measuring about twenty inches long! That's much bigger than a human's tongue, which is only about three and a half inches. And the part of the tongue that sticks out when they're eating is purple! The dark color helps protect it from getting sunburned.

That long tongue comes in handy when trying to eat the leaves and bark of the giraffe's favorite tree, the acacia (say: uh-**kay**-shuh). These trees grow in the African grasslands where giraffes live.

Giraffes can spend twelve hours a day eating. That's why their tongues need the natural purple sunscreen! They eat about seventy-five pounds of food each day. But they don't have to wash all that food down with lots of water. Giraffes get most of their water from the leaves they eat. They only stop to drink water once every two or three days.

This giraffe's tummy is full. She'd like to relax, but first she stretches her long neck and looks around for predators. Nearby, a lion is hiding. He thinks the giraffe would make a delicious meal.

The giraffe lets out a snort to warn others about the lion and runs away—super fast!

Both her front legs move forward. Then her back legs move forward and swing past her front legs. A giraffe can run up to thirty-five miles an hour.

Now that the giraffe is safe, she slows down. Her legs move differently when she's not running. While walking, she takes a step forward with both legs on one side and then moves both legs on the other side.

The giraffe has met up with her herd, also called a tower. Most towers are made up of ten to twenty giraffes, but some can have as many as fifty giraffes.

The tower has a new member: A calf was born.
The baby giraffe is curled up on the ground. She
might be a baby, but she's already six feet tall!

Even though the calf was just born a few hours ago, she is up on her feet and walking. The tower is on the move.

The giraffes stop at a watering hole—but their necks aren't long enough to reach the water! They must either spread their front legs out wide or bend their knees. Only then are they able to lower their heads down to the water.

Since the giraffes are in an awkward position, they don't all drink at the same time. As some drink, others watch for predators.

The calf cuddles up to her mama. Look closely at their spots. They look similar, but they aren't exactly the same. Every giraffe has a different pattern, just like every human has a different fingerprint!

Their spots don't just look pretty; they also keep them safe. Blood vessels underneath the spots help release heat so giraffes don't get too hot under the African sun. And the spots act as camouflage, blending in with the trees and bushes to keep giraffes hidden from their enemies.

In 2023, at a zoo in Tennessee, a baby giraffe was born with no spots at all. This is thought to be the only spotless giraffe in the entire world! Her name is Kipekee (say: key-**peh**-kay), which means "unique" in Swahili.

Look! A fight has broken out between two young males. But don't worry—they are only practicing their fighting skills. Giraffes can use their long, strong necks to protect themselves.

It is rare for giraffes to fight each other, but when they do, watch out! The thick bumps on the top of the male's head, called ossicones, can injure an opponent.

Female giraffes have ossicones, too, but theirs are thin and hairy. And female giraffes rarely fight!

Each year, the giraffe population gets smaller. Why is this happening? Because people are cutting down the trees in their habitat—the place where they live.

Fewer trees mean less food for the giraffes. Without trees, giraffes will starve. Sadly, there are only about 117,000 giraffes left in the wild today.

It has been a long day. The giraffes want to get some sleep. The baby lies down and tucks her legs under her body. Then she uses her backside as a comfy pillow!

But it is too hard for the mama to get to the ground.
After all, it's a long, long way down! So the mama
closes her eyes and takes a quick nap standing up. Most
giraffes only get about thirty minutes of sleep a day.

Giraffes are tall.
Giraffes are fast.
Giraffes are beautiful.
To make a long story short,

giraffes are amazing!